The Story of the
CONSTITUTION

By Marilyn Prolman

Illustrated by Robert Glaubke

 CHILDRENS PRESS, CHICAGO

Library of Congress Catalog Card Number: 69-14680

10 11 12 13 14 15 16 17 18 19 20 21 R

On the Eighth of July, 1776, the big iron bell in the tower at Philadelphia rang out. The Declaration of Independence had been signed. It said, "These united colonies are, and of a right ought to be, free and independent states."

This was during the Revolutionary War. At first, the colonists had been fighting for their rights as Englishmen. As the war progressed, however, the idea of independence grew. With the signing of the Declaration of Independence, a new and independent nation was born. When the Declaration was read to the people, they cheered and sang. The thirteen colonies had thrown off the rule of Great Britain.

The colonies worked together until the war was won. Then they became again almost like thirteen little separate countries. They had won their freedom and independence from England. Now each had its own interests. Each state made its own laws. Each made its own money. Each had its own way of taxing. The people of the colonies did not even call themselves Americans. They were New Yorkers, Virginians, Pennsylvanians. They had not yet learned to be united. They had not yet learned to work together.

They did know that if they were to be one nation they had to have a central government. A group was organized to draw up a plan of government called the Articles of Confederation. It took four years before all the states agreed. At last, in 1781, all thirteen states had signed the Articles.

Upon hearing this news, John Paul Jones fired a twenty-one-gun salute from his ship *Ariel*, moored at

Philadelphia. However, there were very few public celebrations. People were too concerned about their own affairs. Also, news between the states traveled slowly in those days. It had to be carried by sailing ship up the coast, or overland by stagecoach or horseman.

Even though there were few fireworks when the Articles were signed, it was an exciting experiment in government. Most countries were ruled by kings. The idea of people making their own laws was a brand new one. There was no other government like this in the world.

Great as it was as an idea, the Articles were not strong enough to work properly. There were several things wrong. Each state, wanting to be free and independent, had insisted on its own right to make decisions. This meant that the central government had little power. There was no executive head of these united states. Even though laws could be passed, they could not be enforced. The central government had no troops. The country was in debt from the war. The central government could ask for money from the states, but it could not make them obey. Despite these problems, the government of the new little nation limped along for five years.

The years under the Articles of Confederation were interesting times for America.

Philadelphia was a busy, beautiful city. It had some paved streets and many whale-oil street lamps.

Williamsburg was a charming college town, center of the social life of the people who lived on the great plantations in Virginia.

Baltimore, Annapolis, Boston, New York — each had a personality and life of its own. Most travel was by river or sea because even within the seaboard states there were great wilderness areas.

Land of this new nation extended to the Mississippi River and from the Ohio River to Canada. Most of this land, west of the mountains, was forest wilderness. Land companies sprang up. They bought up millions of acres of land for speculation.

It was during this period that twenty-five-year-old Noah Webster wrote his blue-backed speller and his first school reader. John Fitch was experimenting with a steamboat. In 1786 his boat moved up the Delaware River at three miles an hour driven by twelve mechanical oars. Industry was growing up north. Tobacco and cotton flourished in the south.

With this growth, the problems of not having a strong central government began to appear.

The nation was expanding. Many settlers had followed Daniel Boone into Kentucky over the trail he had cut through the Cumberland Gap. Land was being cleared. Farms were being established.

There were many fine colleges in the colonies. Harvard was already one hundred fifty years old. However, lower grade schools were too few. Most children were taught at home or in groups by the local preacher.

In spite of the rapid growth of industry, there were money problems. Each state and the central government printed its own money. A man from Virginia did not want to sell his cotton to a man with New York money. A farmer in Pennsylvania wanted Pennsylvanian money for his crops. He was not certain if the money from another state was safe. Soon only gold and silver had any real value.

Some farmers in Massachusetts found that they could not even pay their taxes with the paper money they had received as soldiers in the Revolution. Under the leadership of Daniel Shays, they marched in revolt against the government of Massachusetts.

Massachusetts called for help from the congress. But congress had no help to send. Eventually Shays'

Rebellion was put down without the help of the central government, but there was one important and immediate result. It finally brought to the attention of the people the need for a stronger central government. "We must do something," they said. "The Articles must be fixed or the nation can't grow."

In 1786 all the states were notified that a meeting or convention would be held the next year to fix the

Articles of Confederation. All thirteen states were to send their representatives to the State House in Philadelphia.

On the second Monday in May, 1787, delegates began arriving in Philadelphia. They came by boat, by stagecoach, and by horseback. Travel was slow and difficult so that it was eleven days before enough men were present to begin the meetings. Twelve states sent delegates. Only Rhode Island sent no representative.

Fifty-five men finally went to work behind closed doors of the State House. What an amazing group of patriots they were! Some had fought in the Revolution. Many had worked in government. All were well educated.

Six of them were only in their twenties. George Washington, who was in his fifties, came from Mount Vernon where he had retired to take care of his

plantation. Alexander Hamilton was thirty. James Madison was only thirty-six. But despite his youth, Madison's work during the convention was to earn him the title "Father of the Constitution." Benjamin Franklin who lived in Philadelphia was eighty-one, but he had the active mind of a young man. All were eager to repair the Articles so that their new country would continue to grow strong.

George Washington was elected president of the meeting. Very shortly it became clear that the Articles of Confederation could not be used. A completely new plan of government had to be written. So they went to work to write the Constitution of the United States. How it was to be organized they did not know. They followed the advice of John Dickinson, "Experience must be our only guide. Reason may mislead us."

They agreed on the reasons for writing the Constitution. They wanted the states to get along together. They called this "domestic tranquility." They wanted the country to be able to defend itself. They wanted to secure liberty for themselves and their children.

There were many things they did not agree on, however. Hamilton wanted the president and legislators elected for life.

"But that would be like having a king," someone shouted. "We have had enough of kings!"

"Small states should have as much to say in making laws as big states," some argued.

Others felt that the largest states should have the largest voice.

Washington, Madison, and Franklin favored a strong national government. Many others did not.

The small states thought they would be overshadowed by the big states. Tempers flared. But wise men worked as the hot days of summer dragged by. It took all summer to draft the seven articles of the Constitution. Their agreement became known as "the Great Compromise."

First they dealt with the people's voice in governing themselves. In Article I of the Constitution, they agreed on the law-making, or legislative branch of the government. They decided that Congress would be made up of two houses. In the Senate, each state, regardless of size, would send two senators. In the

House of Representatives, the number of representatives would be based on population. This compromise satisfied both large and small states. Because no law could become law unless it was passed by both houses, each would have their say.

They stated that Congress can levy taxes for defense and general welfare . . . coin money . . . fix standards of weights and measures . . . establish post offices. Then, to keep Congress from having too much power, they said that no bill will become law until the President signs it. If he does not, the bill has to go back and be approved by two-thirds majority of both houses.

Article II defined the executive branch. It says one man, the President, will be head of the government. He would be elected for a four-year term. The President will see that laws are enforced; be commander in chief of the Armed Forces; he will suggest steps that Congress should take because of needs of the country.

To prevent the President from having too much power, Article II states that he will do some things only with the advice of the Senate:

Appoint judges to the Supreme Court.

Appoint ambassadors.

Make treaties with foreign countries.

In Article III, the delegates organized the Supreme
Court, the judicial branch of the government. They
gave Congress the power to set up other small courts
under the Supreme Court. The Supreme Court was
given authority to handle all cases that have to do
with the Constitution or laws of the United States.
It was to be the highest court in the land. Nine
judges, appointed by the President and approved by
Congress, would sit in this court.

These first three articles set up the form of the federal government. It would be the supreme law of the land. States were free to make their own laws as long as they did not disagree with the federal laws.

Once the form of government was agreed upon, the delegates wrote four more articles. These four articles defined the rights and privileges of the states and the central government.

Relationship of states is handled in Article IV. It provides that all states shall honor the laws of the other states. Citizens of one state shall enjoy the rights of citizens in all states. The United States government will protect each state against invasion and violence.

The wise men writing the Constitution had faith in this new country called the United States of America. They knew that it would grow. With growth comes change. In Article V, how to change, or amend, the Constitution, they wrote that when two-thirds of both houses of Congress—or two-thirds of all the states—think it is needed, an amendment to the Constitution will be considered. In either case, it cannot become law until it is ratified or approved by three-fourths of all the states.

Article VI states, the new government will pay all debts against the country. The Constitution and all treaties shall be the supreme law of the land. All members of Congress and of the state legislatures must support the Constitution as the supreme law of the land. No person shall have to take a religious test to qualify for public office.

Finally, they had to agree on how and when this new Constitution would become law.

Article VII states, that the Constitution shall become law when conventions of nine of the thirteen states have ratified it.

The hot summer of 1787 drew to a close. The seven

articles of the Constitution had been agreed upon. Gouverneur Morris carefully wrote it out by hand and it was signed "by the unanimous consent of the states present" on the seventeenth day of September, in the year of our Lord one thousand seven hundred and eighty-seven and of the Independence of the United States the twelfth."

Benjamin Franklin looked at the half sun on the back of Washington's chair and said, "At length I have the happiness to know that it is a rising and not a setting sun."

The United States had a new form of government. But it now had to have the support of the people. Nine states must ratify it before it could become law.

The states called meetings to discuss this new Constitution and the arguments began again. Finally, by July, 1788, nine states had ratified the Constitution as it had been written in Philadelphia. Massachusetts and Maryland signed it with the understanding that changes would be considered.

George Washington was elected President in 1789. By June of the following year, all thirteen states had ratified the Constitution. The first Congress considered many changes, but only ten amendments were added to the original Constitution. These ten amend-

ments became known as the Bill of Rights, because they defined the rights of the people . . . freedom of religion, of speech, of the press, of peaceful assembly. They also guaranteed privacy and the rights of persons accused of crimes.

Almost two hundred years later, only fifteen more amendments have been added to the Constitution.

The fifty-five wise men who met in Philadelphia in 1787 can be proud of the work they did. They designed a completely new form of government when they wrote the Constitution of the United States. Perhaps the secret of their success was their unshakable faith in the future. As Gouverneur Morris expressed it, "Surely those who come after us will judge better of things present, than we can judge of things future." Accordingly, they left out the details and provided just a basic framework for the government. And the Constitution, often called "a bundle of compromises," has worked better than any of its planners could have foreseen.

The Three Branches of

EXECUTIVE BRANCH (Enforces laws)

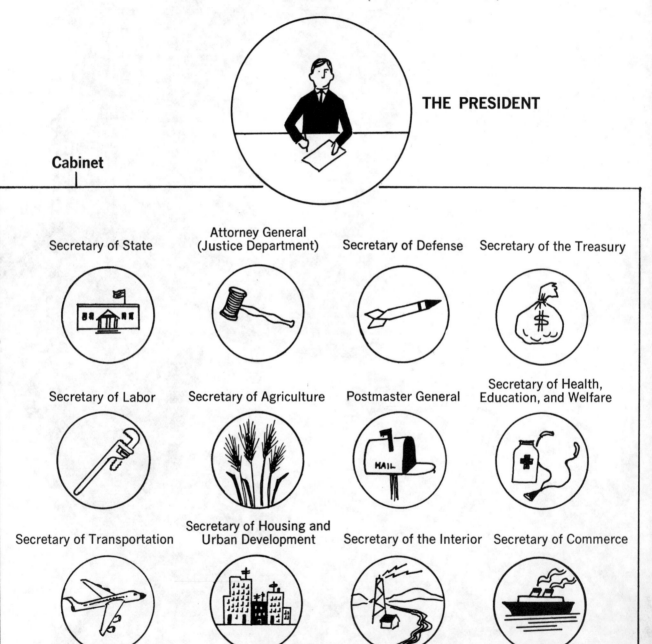

THE PRESIDENT

Cabinet

Secretary of State

Attorney General
(Justice Department)

Secretary of Defense

Secretary of the Treasury

Secretary of Labor

Secretary of Agriculture

Postmaster General

Secretary of Health,
Education, and Welfare

Secretary of Transportation

Secretary of Housing and
Urban Development

Secretary of the Interior

Secretary of Commerce

the Federal Government

LEGISLATIVE BRANCH (Makes laws)

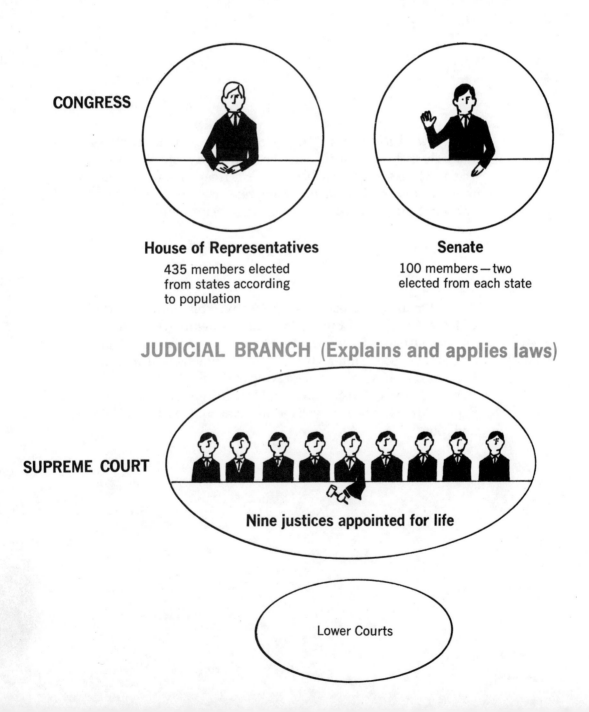

CONGRESS

House of Representatives

435 members elected
from states according
to population

Senate

100 members—two
elected from each state

JUDICIAL BRANCH (Explains and applies laws)

SUPREME COURT

Nine justices appointed for life

Lower Courts

About the Author: Marilyn Prolman was born in Boston, Massachusetts. She attended the University of Wisconsin where she majored in English. She is a free-lance writer and has written several books for young readers. A mid-westerner by choice, she has lived in Chicago since her graduation.

About the Artist: Robert Glaubke received his training at the Chicago Academy of Fine Arts and is now employed there as an art instructor. He works also as a free-lance illustrator and author. His special interests are history, Indians, and animals. Combat sketches made while serving in the South Pacific with the 4th Marine Division were published in a Chicago newspaper. Mr. Glaubke now lives in Evanston with his wife and son.